MVFOL

# Endangered Animals

## Words by Dean Morris

Raintree Childrens Books

Milwaukee • Toronto • Melbourne • London

Library of Congress Number: 77-8365

        6  7  8  9  0  85  84  83

Printed and bound in the United States of America.

Library of Congress Cataloging in Publication Data

Morris, Dean.
    Endangered animals.

    (Read about)
    Includes index.
    SUMMARY: A survey of the various species
endangered by humans with a discussion of what is
being done to preserve these animals from extinction.
    1.  Rare animals — Juvenile literature.  [1.  Rare
animals.  2.  Wildlife preservation]  I.  Title.
QL83.M67   591'.04'2   77-8365
ISBN 0-8393-0011-5

This book has been reviewed
for accuracy by

Dr. Max Allen Nickerson
Head, Vertebrate Division
Milwaukee Public Museum

# Endangered
# Animals

You will never see these animals in a zoo. They were alive millions of years ago, long before people lived on earth. The weather was slowly changing. So were the plants that the animals ate. The animals could not live in the changing world. They died out.

dodo

great
auk

passenger
pigeon

These animals have all died out too.
Too many of them were killed by people.
The dodo and great auk could not fly.
It was easy for hunters to kill them.
Passenger pigeons were killed for sport.
Quaggas were hunted for their skins.
People killed Irish elk for their antlers.

quagga

great Irish elk

Other animals are endangered today.
They need forests, marshes, and prairies
for their food and shelter. People
cut down trees and shrubs. They drain
marshes and clear spaces to build homes
and to raise crops. The animals have
nowhere to go.

Sometimes animals die because of
poisons in the water and air. Sometimes
they die because people hunt them for
sport, food, or skins. People have made
it difficult for animals to find safe places
to live. Many kinds of animals are
becoming rare.

jaguar

tapir

tamarin

These animals may
live in rain forests
or jungles. They find
food and shelter there.

More people
causes the need to
raise more food.
People clear rain
forests to plant
crops. Then the rain
forest animals must
try to survive somewhere
else. Many of them die.

Koala bears feed on eucalyptus tree leaves. People want to get wood from the eucalyptus trees. Many are being cut down. Others are burned in forest fires.

The koalas need these trees, or they will die.

koala

brant goose

Brant geese feed on eelgrass. Dams are going up on the streams where eelgrass grows. Brants might die out too.

Even animals that live in the ocean are in danger.

Coral reefs are made up of the remains of thousands of tiny animals. Many fish make their homes in the reefs.

Starfish eat the coral reefs. Trumpet shells eat some starfish. People collect the trumpet shells.

Can you guess what happens? In some places not enough trumpet shells are left to eat the starfish. More and more starfish are eating the coral reefs. Some reefs may become too small. The reef fish and other reef animals may have no place to live.

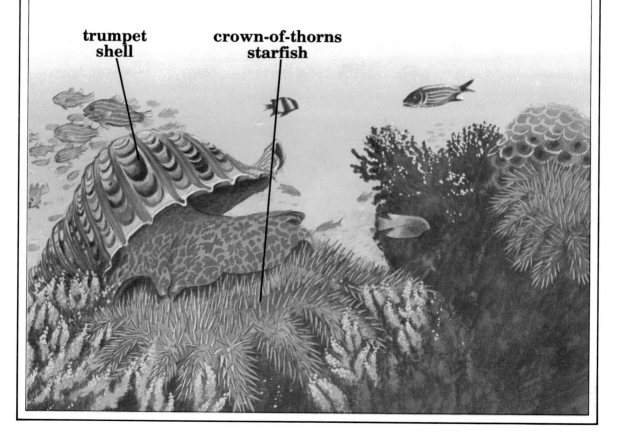

**trumpet shell**

**crown-of-thorns starfish**

Many whales are becoming rare. Today people use big ships and planes with radar to find whales. They kill the whales with large spears called harpoons.

Many things are made from whales. But people are killing too many whales. Soon there may be none left.

**dog food**

**perfume**

**film**

**soap**

**paint**

**harpoon gun**

**fin whale**

People destroy wilderness areas and put the lives of birds in danger. Some people shoot birds for sport. Others hunt for birds' eggs to eat. Some people collect eggs. They take them from the birds' nests. The eggs cannot hatch without the mother bird. Fewer baby birds are born.

Many kinds of birds are becoming rare.

guillemot

Manx shearwater

puffin

kite

Have you ever
felt a fur coat or sat
on a rug made from a
zebra's skin? Many
animals have been
killed so that people
could have clothing
and rugs made of
animal skins.

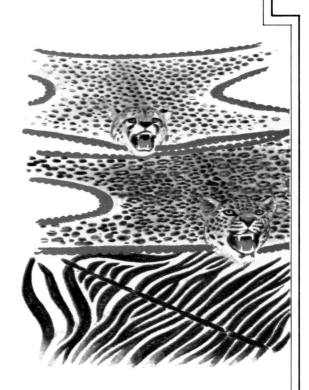

Birds of paradise
have beautiful
feathers. People kill
the birds to get their
colorful feathers.

In the United States, big herds of buffalo used to live on the plains. Indians hunted the buffalo for food and skins. They usually killed only as many as they needed.

When railroads were built across the plains, the buffalo were hunted to feed the people who worked on the railroads. Many other people killed the buffalo just for fun.

Now wild buffalo are very rare.

Pollution kills many animals too. Pollution is anything that makes the air, the earth, or water harmful or undesirable to living things.

Ships that carry oil sometimes have accidents. The oil spills into the sea. Underwater oil wells may have leaks too. Many plants and animals may be destroyed or damaged. Seabirds get covered with the oil. It makes their wings too heavy to fly. They cannot get food. Many of them die.

Waste from factories sometimes gets into rivers. It poisons the fish and other aquatic life.

Farmers spray plants to kill insects. Other animals, like birds, eat the insects that have been poisoned. The poison may cause the birds' eggs to have thin shells. The shells are weak. They have cracks. Baby birds cannot grow inside them.

**peregrine falcon**

frigate
bird

goat

albatross

giant
tortoise

blue-footed
booby

rat

18

Long ago, sailors visited the Galapagos Islands in the Pacific Ocean. They brought goats with them. The goats ate almost all the plants within reach. Some island animals cannot reach the higher plants. They cannot get enough food.

Rats came ashore from the ships too. Rats eat birds' eggs and small animals. Now there are fewer birds and other animals.

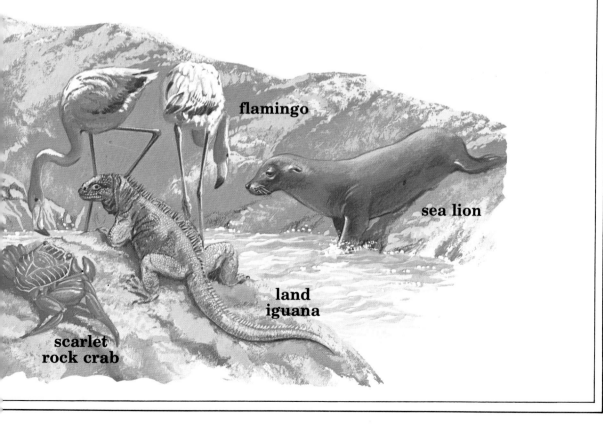

flamingo

sea lion

land iguana

scarlet rock crab

Scientists use some monkeys to test medicines. They give the monkeys new drugs. They want to see if the drugs will work on people. Many animals have been caught for this use. Some kinds of monkeys are becoming rare.

Orangutans are rare animals. Hunters try to capture young orangutans. In the past, hunters could sell the animals to zoos.

A mother orangutan may fight to protect her baby. Often hunters must kill the mother to take a live baby. In the past baby orangutans were rarely born in zoos. Few orangutans are left in the wild.

sable
antelope

wildebeest

zebra

hippopotamus

What can people do to save all these
endangered animals? In many countries,
land is set aside. Animals are protected
in their natural homes.

elephant

rhinoceros

lions

In wildlife reserves, animals are not kept in cages. They are free to roam. People come and see the animals. They cannot feed them or shoot them.

If a reserve gets too crowded, some animals are moved. This is how some big animals are moved: First someone shoots the animal with a dart. The dart holds a drug that makes the animal sleepy. The conservation agents tie the animal's legs. The agents protect the animal's head with padding. Then they load the animal on a truck.

This rhinoceros will be moved to a new home on another reserve.

zebra

Scientists study how animals and birds move from place to place. They put a special mark on each animal. The animal can be identified if it is found later.

bird banding

Some reserves are kept just for birds.
These are places where birds can be safe
when they lay their eggs. No one may
touch the nests or steal the eggs. The
young birds are protected too.

herring gull

black-headed gull

marsh harrier

goldfinch

curlew

ruff

avocet

pintail

lapwing

eider duck

Everglades National Park is a wildlife reserve in Florida. Parts of the Everglades are wet and swampy. People travel by boat to look at the animals there.

Now the swamps around the Everglades are being drained. People want to build houses there. Draining the swamps could dry out the Everglades. Many people are working to keep this from happening.

Because of wildlife reserves, many kinds
of animals have been saved. In Russia too
many saigas were hunted. They almost
died out. The Russians put the saigas
on special reserves. Many young were
born. Today there are large herds of
these animals.

saiga

A Chinese ruler used to keep rare deer in his park for hunting. A man called Père David saw the animals. He wanted to make sure the deer did not die out. He sent some to zoos where more could be born. This kind of deer is named for Père David.

Père David's deer

Wild horses are protected because so few of them are left.

Nenes are kept on reserves too. Many young nenes are sent to Hawaii. That is where they first lived.

nene

The biggest wildlife reserve of all is the Antarctic region. Only a few kinds of animals live in this cold place. Those that do live there are often found in great numbers. They are safe there.

albatross

king penguins

elephant seal

leopard seal

The first people who went to the Antarctic hunted the seals. Soon only a few were left. Then many countries agreed not to hunt in the Antarctic any more. Now there are many seals. Penguins and other animals are safe there too.

Animals that live near the South Pole often find food in the sea at the edge of the ice.

snow petrel

southern
fulmar

Weddell
seal

cormorant

Few of us get the chance to visit a wildlife reserve. But we can all see rare animals in some zoos.

Not all animals are kept in cages. Many zoos have open places like the animals' natural homes.

Zoo keepers try to breed the wild
animals at the zoo. Some of the young
animals are returned to the wild. This
may help save some of the endangered
animals for the future.

# Where to Read About
# the Endangered Animals

**seal** (sēl) *pp. 30, 31*

**snow petrel** (snō pe′ trəl) *p. 31*

**southern fulmar** (su<u>th</u>′ ərn fool′ mər)
*p. 31*

**starfish** (stär′ fish′) *p. 11*

**tamarin** (tam′ ə rən) *p. 8*

**tapir** (tā′ pər) *p. 8*

**tiger** (tī′ gər) *p. 33*

**tortoise** (tôr′ təs) *p. 18*

**trumpet shell** (trum′ pit shel) *p. 11*

**Weddell seal** (wə del′ sēl) p. 31

**whale** (hwāl) *p. 12*

**wildebeest** (wil′ də bēst′) *p. 22*

# Pronunciation Key for Glossary

| | |
|---|---|
| a | a as in **cat**, **bad** |
| ā | a as in **able**, ai as in **train**, ay as in **play** |
| ä | a as in **father**, **car** |
| e | e as in **bend**, **yet** |
| ē | e as in **me**, ee as in **feel**, ea as in **beat**, ie as in **piece**, y as in **heavy** |
| i | i as in **in**, **pig** |
| ī | i as in **ice**, **time**, ie as in **tie**, y as in **my** |
| o | o as in **top** |
| ō | o as in **old**, oa as in **goat**, ow as in **slow**, oe as in **toe** |
| ô | o as in **cloth**, au as in **caught**, aw as in **paw**, a as in **all** |
| oo | oo as in **good**, u as in **put** |
| o͞o | oo as in **tool**, ue as in **blue** |
| oi | oi as in **oil**, oy as in **toy** |
| ou | ou as in **out**, ow as in **plow** |
| u | u as in **up**, **gun**, o as in **other** |
| ur | ur as in **fur**, er as in **person**, ir as in **bird**, or as in **work** |
| yo͞o | u as in **use**, ew as in **few** |
| ə | a as in **again**, e as in **broken**, i as in **pencil**, o as in **attention**, u as in **surprise** |
| ch | ch as in **such** |
| ng | ng as in **sing** |
| sh | sh as in **shell**, **wish** |
| th | th as in **three**, **bath** |
| <u>th</u> | th as in **that**, **together** |

# GLOSSARY

These words are defined the way they are used in this book.

**accident** (ak′ sə dənt) something that happens that is not expected

**antler** (ant′ lər) one of the two branched horns on the head of a deer, elk, or moose

**aquatic** (ə′ kwät ik) growing or living in water

**area** (er′ ē ə) the surface within a certain boundary; a certain space, region, or section

**ashore** (ə shôr′) on or to the land

**aside** (ə sīd′) on or to one side

**build** (bild) to make by putting things together

**built** (bilt) see **build**

**cannot** (kan′ ot *or* ka not′) can not; not able

**Chinese** (chī nez′) having to do with the country of China

**collect** (kə lekt′) to gather together

**colorful** (kul′ ər fəl) having a lot
of color; full of color

**conservation agent** (kon sər vā′ shən
ā′ jənt) a person who watches over and
protects the forests, animals, rivers,
minerals, and other natural resources
of an area

**capture** (kap′ chər) to catch and hold
something

**coral reef** (kôr′ əl rēf) a ridge that
usually lies at or near the surface of
the ocean that is made up of the skeletons
of tiny sea animals

**crop** (krop) plants that are grown to be
used for food or something else used
by people

**damage** (dam′ ij) to harm or injure

**dart** (därt) a sharp pointed object that
looks like a small arrow

**destroy** (di stroi′) to ruin completely

**drain** (drān) to empty all the liquid
from something

**drug** (drug) a substance, usually a chemical,

that makes a change in the body

**eelgrass** (ēl' grās) an aquatic plant that
has very long narrow leaves

**endangered** (en dān' jərd) to put in
danger of becoming extinct

**eucalyptus** (yōō' kə lip' təs) tall trees
that grow mostly in the country
of Australia

**extinct** (eks tingkt') no longer living
or found on earth

**factory** (fak' tər ē) a building or
group of buildings where things are made

**harmful** (härm' fəl) causing damage or
harm

**harpoon** (här pōōn') a weapon that looks
like a spear and has a rope attached to it

**hatch** (hach) to come from an egg

**herd** (hurd) a group of animals

**identify** (i den' tə fī') to show that
something is what you say it is

**Indian** (in' dē ən) a member of one of
the tribes living in North and South
America

**insect** (in' sekt) a small animal without a backbone, such as a fly or ant

**jungle** (jung' gəl) land in warm, damp places covered with many trees, vines, and bushes

**leak** (lēk) a hole or tear in something that lets something else pass through by accident

**marsh** (märsh) an area of low, wet land

**medicine** (med' ə sin) a drug or other material which is used to cure sickness or relieve pain

**million** (mil' yən) the number 1,000,000

**natural** (nach' ər əl) found in nature; not made by people

**nowhere** (nō' hwer') not any place

**oil** (oil) a greasy substance that does not mix with water

**padding** (pad' ing) a piece of soft, thick material

**plain** (plān) an area of flat land

**poison** (poi' zən) something that can cause sickness or death

**pollution** (pə lo͞o′ shən) something that makes something else dirty or impure

**prairie** (prer′ ē) an area of land that is usually flat and covered with grass without many trees

**radar** (rā′ dar) a device or system used to find and follow objects by means of radio waves

**railroad** (rāl′ rōd′) the tracks, cars, and stations that make up a system of transportation

**rare** (rer) not often found or seen; not common

**rat** (rat) an animal that looks like a mouse but is bigger

**region** (rē′ jən) a large area or territory

**remains** (ri mānz′) a dead body; what is left behind

**reserve** (ri zurv′) a special area set aside for the protection of animals and plants

**sailor** (sā′ lər) someone who sails a boat as part of his job

**scientist** (sī′ ən tist) someone who has
studied a great deal about a branch
of science

**seabird** (sē′ burd′) a bird that often
flies over the ocean

**shelter** (shel′ tər) something that covers
or protects

**shrub** (shrub) a woody plant with many
branches close to the ground

**skin** (skin) the outer covering of an
animal or person

**someone** (sum′ wun′) some person; somebody

**somewhere** (sum′ hwer′) in, at, from, or
to an unnamed place

**space** (spās) all the room within an area

**spear** (spēr) a throwing weapon with a
sharp, pointed head attached to a long,
thin handle

**sport** (spôrt) something that is done for fun

**spray** (sprā) to put on a liquid in a fast
stream of small drops

**steal** (stēl) to take something that
belongs to another

**study** (stud′ ē) reading or thinking
about something in order to learn

**survive** (sər vīv′) to continue to exist

**swampy** (swom′ pē) like an area of soft,
wet land

**thousand** (thou′ zənd) the number 1,000

**travel** (trav′ əl) to go from one place
to another

**underwater** (un′ dər wô′ tər) below
the surface of a body of water

**undesirable** (un′ di zīr′ ə bəl)
not pleasing; not worth having

**useful** (yōōs′ fəl) of good use or
purpose; helpful

**weak** (wēk) without power, strength or force

**wild** (wīld) a place where plants and
animals live and grow naturally

**wilderness** (wil′ dər nis) an area where
people have not made homes or lived

**wildlife reserve** (wīld′ līf′  ri zurv′)
a special area where animals
and plants grow naturally and
are protected

**within** (wi<u>th</u> in′ *or* with in′) in or
    into the inside of
**zoo** (zōō) a park or other place where
    people can see animals

# Bibliography

Burton, Maurice, and Burton, Robert, editors.
  *The International Wildlife Encyclopedia.*
  20 vols. Milwaukee: Purnell Reference Books, 1970.

Harris, John, and Pohl, Aleta. *Endangered Predators.*
  New York: Doubleday & Company, 1976.
  Five stories of predatory animals, the wolf,
  fox, coyote, cougar, and bobcat, stressing
  the importance of predators to the balance
  of nature.

Laycock, George. *Wild Refuge.* Garden City,
  N.Y.: Natural History Press, 1969.
  Traces the history of the National Wildlife
  Refuges, describes some of the animals
  which have benefitted from them, and discusses
  the need for increasing wildlife conservation
  efforts.

McCoy, Joseph J. *Saving Our Wildlife.*
  New York: Crowell-Collier Press, 1970.

Sutton, Ann, and Sutton, Myron. *New Worlds
  for Wildlife.* Chicago: Rand McNally, 1970.
  Relates what is being done in one hundred
  countries to save animals from natural and
  man-made disasters and to preserve areas
  for wildlife parks and reserves.